D1709456

High Technology
Virtual Reality

by Julie Murray

Dash!
LEVELED READERS
An Imprint of Abdo Zoom • abdobooks.com

3

3 Dash!
LEVELED READERS

Level 1 – Beginning
Short and simple sentences with familiar words or patterns for children who are beginning to understand how letters and sounds go together.

Level 2 – Emerging
Longer words and sentences with more complex language patterns for readers who are practicing common words and letter sounds.

Level 3 – Transitional
More developed language and vocabulary for readers who are becoming more independent.

THIS BOOK CONTAINS RECYCLED MATERIALS

abdobooks.com

Published by Abdo Zoom, a division of ABDO, PO Box 398166, Minneapolis, Minnesota 55439.
Copyright © 2021 by Abdo Consulting Group, Inc. International copyrights reserved in all countries.
No part of this book may be reproduced in any form without written permission from the publisher.
Dash!™ is a trademark and logo of Abdo Zoom.

Printed in the United States of America, North Mankato, Minnesota.
052020
092020

Photo Credits: Alamy, Getty Images, iStock, Shutterstock, ©Michael Coghlan p.7 / CC BY-SA 2.0
Production Contributors: Kenny Abdo, Jennie Forsberg, Grace Hansen, John Hansen
Design Contributors: Dorothy Toth, Neil Klinepier, Laura Graphenteen

Library of Congress Control Number: 2019956175

Publisher's Cataloging in Publication Data

Names: Murray, Julie, author.
Title: Virtual reality / by Julie Murray
Description: Minneapolis, Minnesota : Abdo Zoom, 2021 | Series: High technology | Includes online
    resources and index.
Identifiers: ISBN 9781098221195 (lib. bdg.) | ISBN 9781098222178 (ebook) | ISBN 9781098222666
    (Read-to-Me ebook)
Subjects: LCSH: Virtual reality--Juvenile literature. | Science--Computer simulation--Juvenile literature. |
    Human-computer interaction--Juvenile literature. | High technology--Juvenile literature. |
    Technological innovations--Juvenile literature.
Classification: DDC 501.13--dc23

Table of Contents

Virtual Reality

Virtual reality (VR) uses technology to create an **artificial** world that feels real.

Products of the past have led to today's VR technology. The View-Master and Sensorama machine are a few early examples.

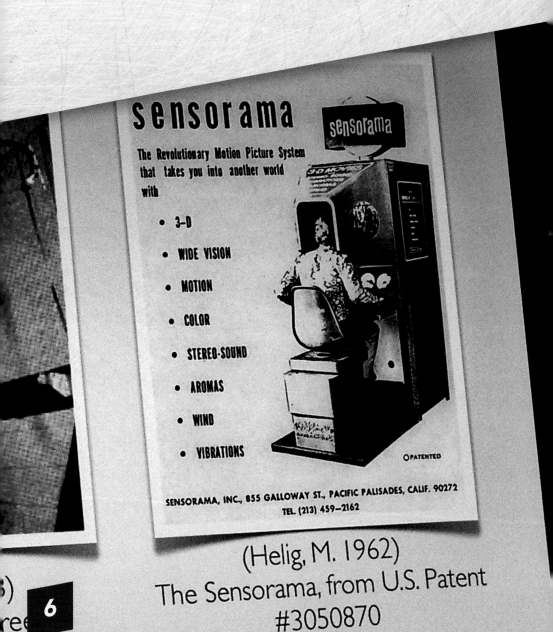

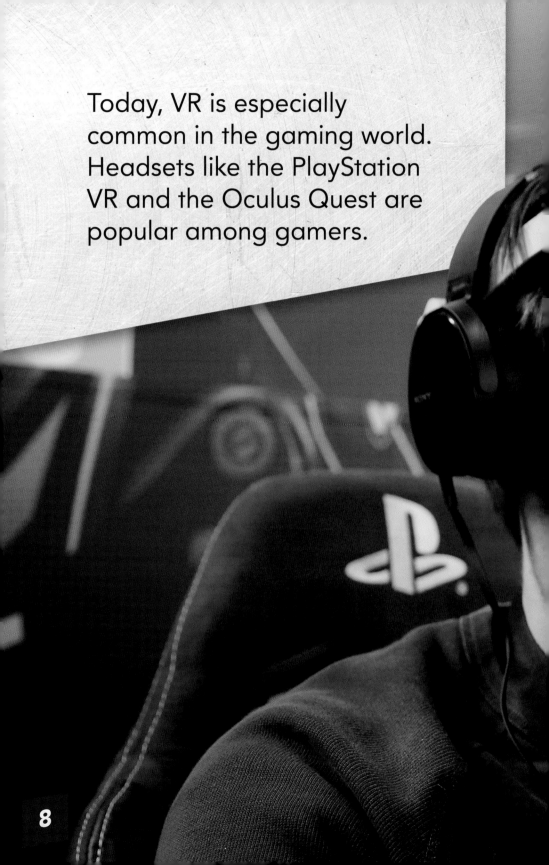

Today, VR is especially common in the gaming world. Headsets like the PlayStation VR and the Oculus Quest are popular among gamers.

How It Works

VR produces images and sounds that make a person feel like they are somewhere else. In VR, a person is able to move around. They can **interact** with a virtual world and it responds back.

Most often, a VR headset is worn to get this experience. It looks like a diving mask, but it has a screen in front.

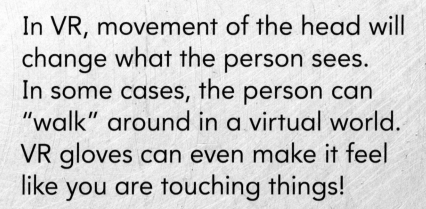

In VR, movement of the head will change what the person sees. In some cases, the person can "walk" around in a virtual world. VR gloves can even make it feel like you are touching things!

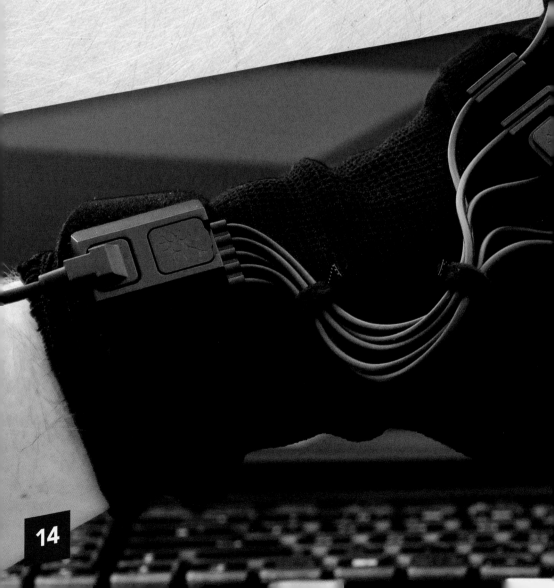

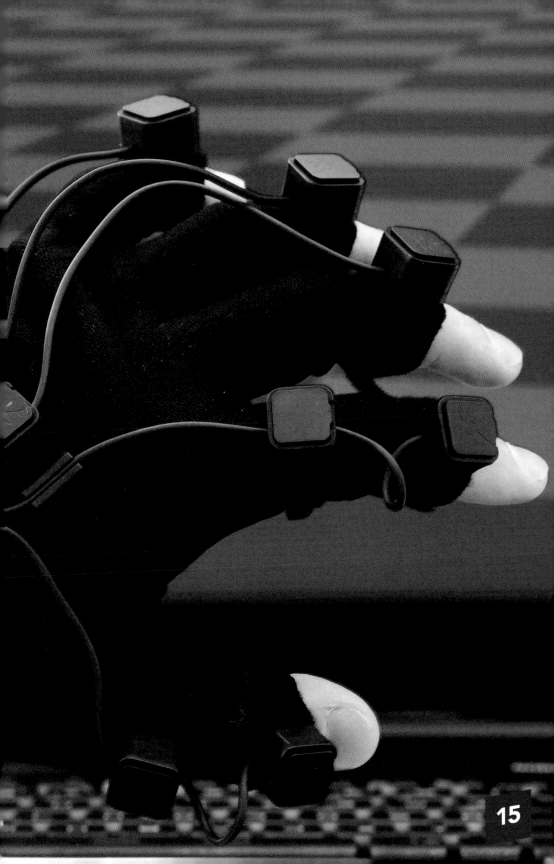

Virtual Reality Uses

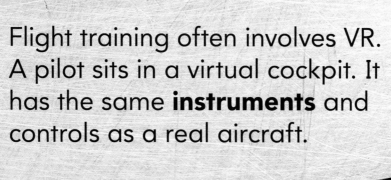

Flight training often involves VR. A pilot sits in a virtual cockpit. It has the same **instruments** and controls as a real aircraft.

Medical doctors also use VR. Many doctors train for **surgical procedures** this way. VR is also used in the military. Soldiers can train for **warfare** using VR.

Many people use VR headsets with their home gaming systems. VR **arcades** are also popping up all over the world.

21

More Facts

- There are VR rooms. These are large rooms with many screens. A person is fully engaged in a virtual world once they step into the room.

- Augmented Reality (AR) is a lot like Virtual Reality (VR). However, VR creates an entirely new universe, while AR overlays virtual elements onto the real world. Like in VR, people can interact with these elements.

- Motion sickness is a common problem with VR. Many people become dizzy and nauseous when using VR.

Glossary

arcade – an indoor space that has multiple video games to play.

artificial – made by human beings.

instrument – a tool or mechanical device used for special work.

interact – to communicate with and respond to one another.

surgical procedure – a medical surgery performed in order to repair the body.

warfare – the act of fighting a war.

Index

Online Resources

Booklinks
NONFICTION NETWORK
FREE! ONLINE NONFICTION RESOURCES

To learn more about virtual reality, please visit **abdobooklinks.com** or scan this QR code. These links are routinely monitored and updated to provide the most current information available.